THE MODERN NERD'S GUIDE TO
ROBOT BATTLES

BY MELISSA RAÉ SHOFNER

 Gareth Stevens
PUBLISHING

Please visit our website, www.garethstevens.com. For a free color catalog of all our high-quality books, call toll free 1-800-542-2595 or fax 1-877-542-2596.

Cataloging-in-Publication Data

Names: Shofner, Melissa Raé.
Title: The modern nerd's guide to robot battles / Melissa Raé Shofner.
Description: New York : Gareth Stevens Publishing, 2018. | Series: Geek out! | Includes index.
Identifiers: LCCN ISBN 9781538212141 (pbk.) | ISBN 9781538212158 (library bound) | ISBN 9781538212189 (6 pack)
Subjects: LCSH: Robots–Design and construction–Juvenile literature. | Robots–Control systems–Juvenile literature. | Robotics–Juvenile literature. | BattleBots (Television program)–Juvenile literature.
Classification: LCC TJ211.S56 2018 | DDC 629.8'92–dc23

First Edition

Published in 2018 by
Gareth Stevens Publishing
111 East 14th Street, Suite 349
New York, NY 10003

Copyright © 2018 Gareth Stevens Publishing

Designer: Sarah Liddell
Editor: Joan Stoltman

Photo credits: Cover, p. 1 Kurita KAKU/Contributor/Gamma-Rapho/Getty Images; texture used throughout StrelaStudio/Shutterstock.com; p. 4 Peter Cade/Iconica/Getty Images; p. 5 AlMare/Wikimedia Commons; p. 7 Claudenw/Wikimedia Commons; p. 9 Pavel L Photo and Video/Shutterstock.com; pp. 11, 13, 19 Jeff Greenberg/Contributor/Universal Images Group/Getty Images; p. 20 digidreamgrafix/Shutterstock.com; p. 21 AlesiaKan/Shutterstock.com; p. 23 ullstein bild/Contributor/ullstein bild/Getty Images; p. 24 ROBYN BECK/Staff/AFP/Getty Images; p. 25 PAUL J. RICHARDS/Contributor/AFP/Getty Images; p. 27 DGLimages/Shutterstock.com; p. 29 BSIP/Contributor/Universal Images Group/Getty Images.

Printed in the United States of America

CPSIA compliance information: Batch #CW18GS: For further information contact Gareth Stevens, New York, New York at 1-800-542-2595.

CONTENTS

Words in the glossary appear in **bold** type the first time they are used in the text.

THE AGE OF ROBOTS

Robots aren't just **science fiction** anymore. People have been **designing** and building robots for hundreds of years! Today, robots are often used to complete tasks that happen over and over many times, are costly, or are unsafe for humans. Robots can be found in auto factories putting together cars or in hospitals performing operations.

Robots can also be a lot of fun! Have you ever heard of robot battles? These are **competitions** in which people design and build robots to combat, or battle against, each other. Combat robots come in all sizes and shapes, and in battle they fight to the finish. May the best robot win!

Robots are machines built by people to do work that's normally done by humans. The science and study of robots is called robotics.

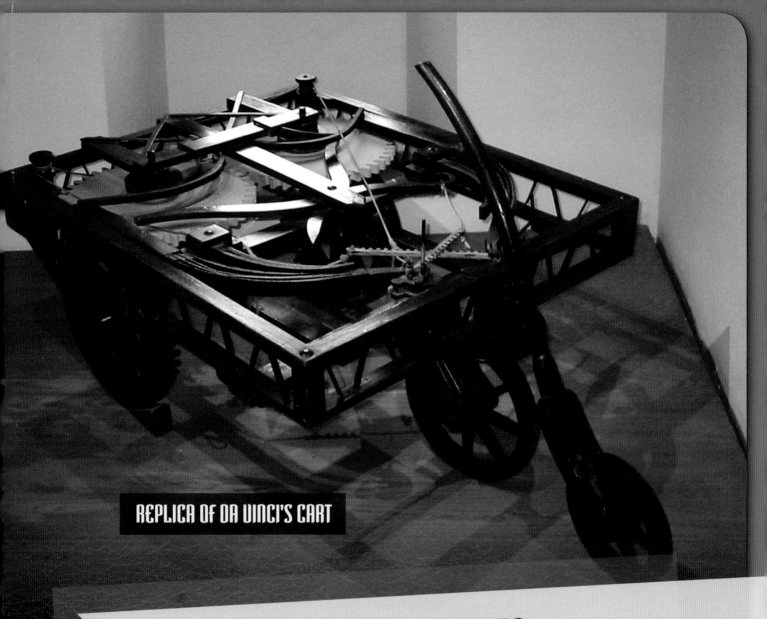

REPLICA OF DA VINCI'S CART

THE FIRST ROBOT?

In the late 1400s, the famous artist and inventor Leonardo da Vinci created a cart that moved by itself using gears, weights, and other special parts. Many people consider this cart to be one of the earliest robots. Drawings of a robotic knight have also been found in da Vinci's notebooks.

IN THE BEGINNING...

The history of robot battles is a little unclear. Some people believe they began when students gathered for **engineering** competitions in the 1970s. Others think they may have started in the 1980s when artists in San Francisco, California, were designing robot bands, circuses, and more!

Many people believe robot combat truly began in 1986 when several engineers formed a group called the Denver Mad Scientists Club. The group organized an event called the Critter Crawl in which members built robots and raced them against each other. After deciding it would be cooler to have the robots fight each other, the group organized a Critter Crunch in 1987.

MAIN EVENTS

Critter Crunch has been held at the MileHiCon science fiction convention, or gathering, since it began in 1987. Robot Battles, a competition based on Critter Crunch's fight rules, was first held in 1991. Robot Wars began in San Francisco in 1994.

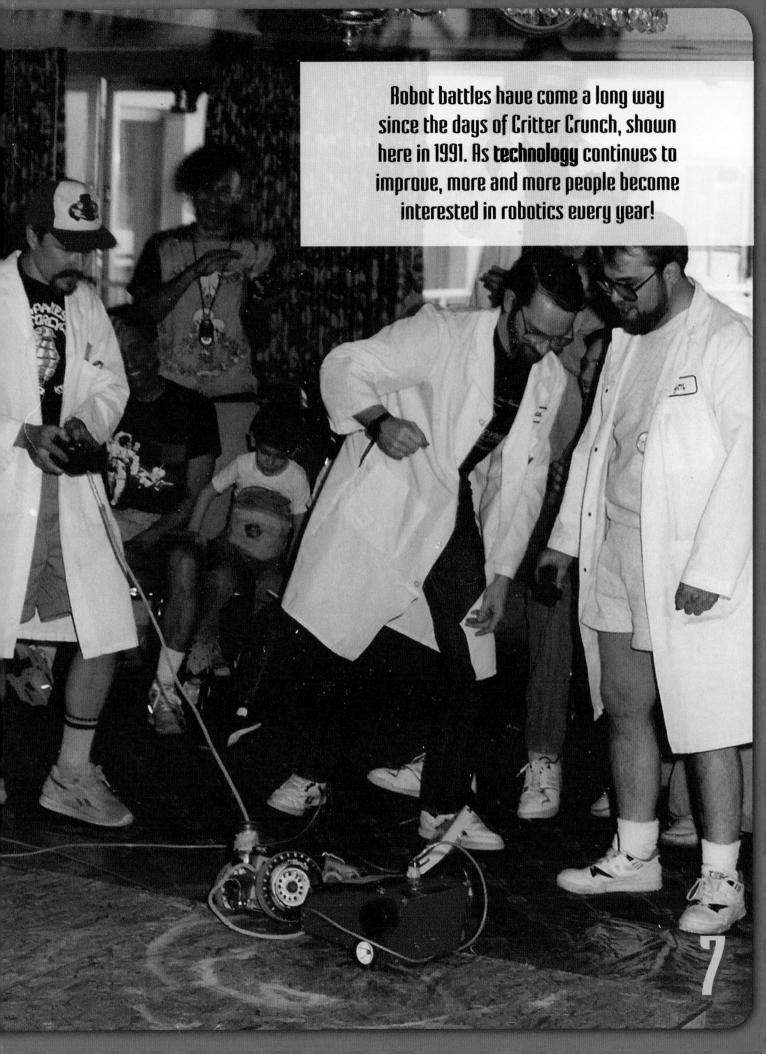

Robot battles have come a long way since the days of Critter Crunch, shown here in 1991. As **technology** continues to improve, more and more people become interested in robotics every year!

BATTLE RULES

In a normal robot battle, two robots fight each other to the finish. They face off in a special combat zone called an arena. Battles consist of a series of 3-minute or 5-minute rounds.

When one of the robots is destroyed or disabled, the round is over. A round may also end if a robot moves outside the combat area or touches an off-limits surface. A robot must win two out of three rounds to be announced the winner. The winning robot gets a small amount of time to be repaired, and then it may go on to fight again.

ALL AROUND THE WORLD

There are organizations around the world that support robot builders and host combat events. Such organizations include the German Roboteers Association, Robowars Australia, and the Dutch Robot Games Foundation. In Europe, the Fighting Robot Association provides a community for robot builders and maintains the rules for building, competing, and judging.

In 2016, special robots called bronebots battled it out in this arena at the Bronebot 2016 Moscow Championship of Fighting Robots in Moscow, Russia. During this battle, several combat robots fought each other at the same time!

A SPORT FOR EVERYONE

One of the coolest things about robot battles is that anyone can **participate**! Unlike many other sports, it doesn't matter how strong or tall or fast you are. Robot battles are all about **creativity**, imagination, and problem solving.

In 2000, a television show called *BattleBots* began airing in the United States. It was a hit and helped create more interest in making robots—especially among young people. In the robot battle world, it doesn't matter how old you are. In 2007, the winner of the 12-pound (5.4 kg) weight class at the StellarCon robot battle in North Carolina was only 9 years old!

FORMING A TEAM

Robots can be designed and built by a single person, but some people prefer to work and compete with a team. Each team member may have a different set of skills. For example, one person may have a strong knowledge of math, and another may be better at skillfully driving the robot.

After *BattleBots* first aired, the official Robot Battles group reached out to schools and colleges to bring in young competitors. At first, *BattleBots* only ran from 2000 to 2002. Then the show was brought back in 2015!

DESIGNING A BATTLE BOT

If you want to build your own combat robot—or any type of robot, really—one of the most important things to remember is to give yourself enough time. Robots often take several months to plan and build. You'll also need time to test your bot, or robot, and fix any issues it may have.

Your battle bot will need a few key parts: a frame, armor, a weapon, a **battery**, a motor, a controller, and a receiver. The controller is what the driver holds to move the robot. The receiver is the special part in the robot that receives messages from the controller on how to move.

GIANT ROBOT BATTLES

The Mk. III is a giant robot called a mech. It's piloted, which means a person actually sits inside it during battle! It was built by MegaBots, Inc. in the United States and stands 16 feet (4.9 m) tall. It weighs 12 tons (10.9 mt) and can even swing a punch!

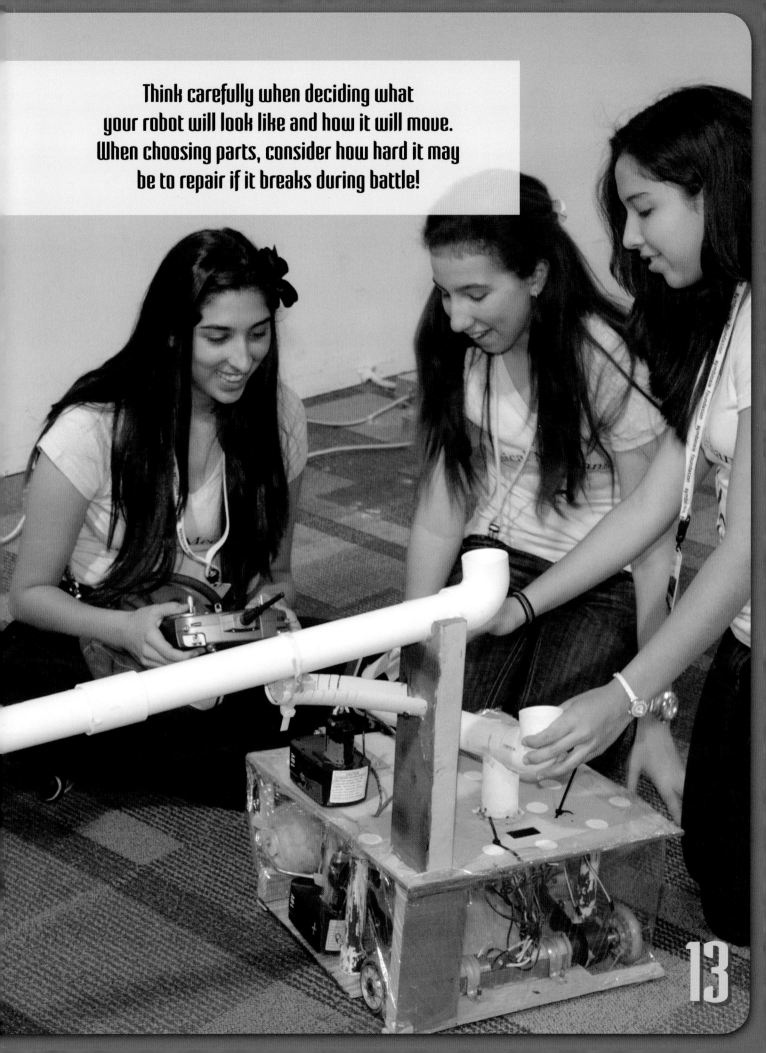

Think carefully when deciding what your robot will look like and how it will move. When choosing parts, consider how hard it may be to repair if it breaks during battle!

13

WEIGHT AND COST

The biggest choices you'll make before a competition are how much to spend and how much your robot will weigh. You'll need to decide what weight class you will be competing in ahead of time. Your design will greatly depend on the weight you choose. Some **materials** are much heavier than others. It sometimes costs more to build using special, lighter materials.

You'll likely have to pay a fee to register for an event. Then you'll need to get you and your robot to the competition, which may be costly if your robot is heavy or if you need to travel far.

A BIG EXPENSE

Building a battle bot can cost between $500 and $70,000—sometimes more! When designing a robot, figure out how much you can spend first. Then shop around for deals on parts. If you're just starting out, get a simple, low-cost robotics kit before spending lots of money on a more **complex** bot.

BATTLEBOTS
WEIGHT CLASSES

WEIGHT CLASS	WEIGHT RANGE WITH WHEELS	WEIGHT RANGE WITH LEGS
SUPERHEAVYWEIGHT	220-340 POUNDS (100-154 KG) WHEELED	264-408 POUNDS (120-185 KG) LEGS
HEAVYWEIGHT	120-220 POUNDS (54-100 KG) WHEELED	144-264 POUNDS (65-120 KG) LEGS
MIDDLEWEIGHT	60-120 POUNDS (27-54 KG) WHEELED	72-144 POUNDS (33-65 KG) LEGS
LIGHTWEIGHT	25-60 POUNDS (11-27 KG) WHEELED	30-72 POUNDS (14-33 KG) LEGS

To help make robot battles fair, robots only battle other robots in their weight class. Weight limits may be slightly different at each competition, so be sure to check the rules before signing up for an event. These are the weight classes only for *BattleBots* events.

CHOOSE YOUR WEAPON

A battle robot's job is to enter the arena and destroy the other robot, called the opponent. To do this, your bot is going to need some weapons! Saws and drills don't have much effect on metal, but they do create cool sparks! Other weapons include hammers, spinning bars, and grabber arms. Read the rules for the competition you want to enter to make sure the weapons you want to use are allowed. Then get creative!

One of the best ways to disable an opponent uses a simple tool that isn't usually used as a weapon at all. A wedge is a simple and effective way to flip over your competition!

WHO MAKES THE RULES?

Rules allow battles to be fought fairly so everyone can enjoy the sport. The Robot Fighting League created a standard set of rules for US events. Recently, the task of creating and maintaining these rules was passed to an organization called SPARC (Standardized Procedures for the Advancement of Robotic Combat).

SOME TYPES OF BATTLE ROBOTS

TYPE OF ROBOT	FEATURES
WEDGE	• PICKS OPPONENT OFF THE FLOOR TO DRIVE INTO A WALL OR OBJECT • HARD TO WRECK • REQUIRES A SKILLED DRIVER
SPINNER	• GETS DAMAGED IN FIGHT, SO YOU'LL NEED LOTS OF SPARE PARTS • TAKES TIME TO REACH FULL SPINNING SPEED • HARD TO DESIGN WELL
DRUM	• THROWS OPPONENTS • HEAVY AND HARD TO CONTROL
CRUSHER	• CAN HOLD AND SOMETIMES BEND OPPONENTS • REQUIRES A SKILLED DRIVER AND GOOD TIMING • SOMETIMES HAS WEIGHT ISSUES DURING DESIGN

These are only some of the many styles of battle robots out there. Maybe when you design a battle robot, you'll combine elements from more than one of these robots!

SAFETY FIRST!

Robot battles are awesome, but there's a lot of danger during an event, too! To keep builders, drivers, judges, and the crowd safe, these events have many important safety rules. For example, battle arenas have a safety zone around them that the crowd needs to stay out of at all times.

Keeping everyone safe starts with how you build your robot. Any robot with weapons needs to have a special feature called a kill switch that will shut off the bot immediately in case something goes wrong. Forcefully thrown weapons, called projectiles, aren't allowed, either.

DON'T BE DISQUALIFIED!

At most events, the judges check robots to be sure they meet the safety rules before allowing them to compete. Being disqualified means you can't compete because you didn't follow the rules. Following the rules allows you and everyone else to have fun without fear of getting hurt!

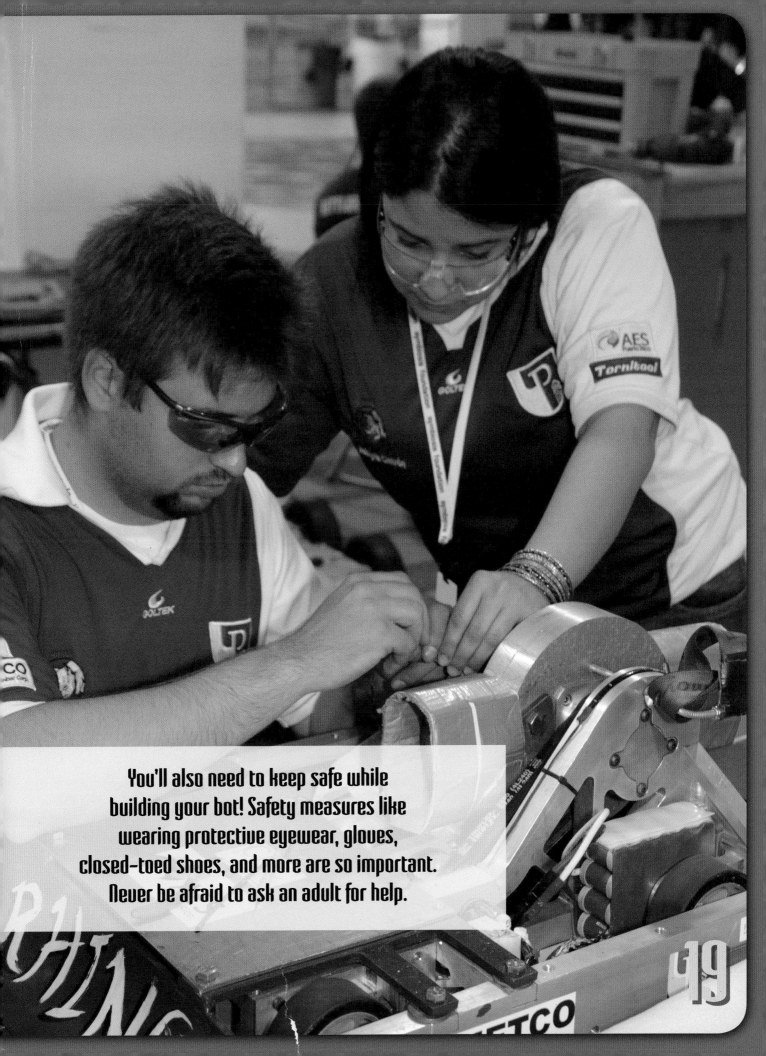

You'll also need to keep safe while building your bot! Safety measures like wearing protective eyewear, gloves, closed-toed shoes, and more are so important. Never be afraid to ask an adult for help.

OTHER ROBOTICS COMPETITIONS

Sumo-style events are popular at many robotics competitions. In a sumo match, two robots go head-to-head in a small, circular arena just like in Japanese sumo wrestling. Without using any weapons and without flipping their opponent, the robots battle to push each other out of the circle.

If you like robots, but aren't interested in battling it out with weapons or in sumo-style battle, there are lots of other robotics competitions out there! Robots can race each other, climb stairs, solve problems, and more. Some events have robots compete in bowling, weight lifting, and firefighting.

Some robotics competitions involve teams of robots that play sports, just like people! These robots are playing hockey. Other popular robot sports are soccer and basketball.

JUST FOR KIDS!

The LEGO company—yes, the one that sells those plastic, colored bricks—is very active in creating chances for young people to try out robotics. They offer special robot-building kits and a variety of classes and after-school programs. LEGO even hosts several competitive robotics leagues just for kids!

LET THE GAMES BEGIN!

If robot battles and other robotics competitions sound like things you may be interested in, there are many ways for you to participate. One of the first things you should do is ask around your school to find out if there are any technology or robotics classes you can take. There are robotics-themed summer camps throughout the United States. Your school may even have a robotics club!

Another place to find out more about robotics is your local library. Some libraries offer robotics classes and have special spaces where you can work on your robot.

JUNIOR LEAGUE FOR YOUNG COMPETITORS

RoboGames encourages people of all ages and skill levels—including children and beginners—to compete. There's even a special Junior League for competitors under 18 years old. Young builders can sign up for Junior League events for free and learn about all RoboGames has to offer.

This robot is working its way through a maze!

23

PARTICIPATING

In 2004, the Robotics Society of America founded a huge competition called the ROBOlympics. The idea behind the event was to get robotics builders to move outside of areas they were already good at by encouraging them to try new robotics events. ROBOlympics also provided an opportunity for builders and the public to see what other people in the robotics community were doing.

Today, the competition is called RoboGames. According to Guinness World Records, it's the biggest open robot competition in the world! More than 70 events are held at the games each year, and people come from around the world to participate.

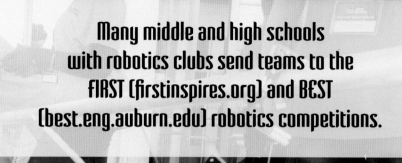

Many middle and high schools
with robotics clubs send teams to the
FIRST (firstinspires.org) and BEST
(best.eng.auburn.edu) robotics competitions.

WHERE TO LEARN MORE

A great way to learn more about robotics
is by attending robot battles and other
types of competitions. These events
are good places to meet builders and
talk to other people who are interested
in robotics. Watching online videos
and reading books and articles about
robotics are other ways to learn and
get new ideas!

THINK LIKE AN ENGINEER

Robot battles are exciting! They're even better when you can take part in the action yourself. You don't need to be fast or strong to build a bot and participate in a robotics competition—these events are truly for everyone. However, to build a successful combat robot, you do need to be able to think like an engineer.

No special skills are required to take up robotics, but you'll find it easier to understand how robots work if you take certain classes in school. Technology and engineering classes are very helpful and can often be taken in high school—and sometimes even middle school.

WHAT IS STEM?

You may have heard the terms "STEM" or "STEAM" at school. STEM and STEAM are a way of teaching through real-life examples that works to build skills in science, technology, engineering, and math. The "A" in "STEAM" adds art and design to the group. Look for classes in your area!

Taking STEM classes in middle and high school can help you build better battle robots. It'll also prepare you for a possible career in robotics in the future!

27

TURNING A HOBBY INTO A CAREER

For many people, robot battles and other types of robot competitions are fun ways to spend their free time. If you participate in these hobbies and find yourself really enjoying them, there are many ways to get paid doing what you love for a living!

Robots are being used in more and more **industries** every day. This means the need for people who are able to design, build, operate, and maintain these robots is on the rise. Many colleges now offer robotics engineering programs to prepare students for these careers. Where can robotics take you?

A WORLD OF OPPORTUNITY

Robots are sometimes used to explore places where people can't go. Scientists have used robots to get a better look inside volcanoes, the deepest parts of the ocean, and even outer space. In the future, tiny robots called nanobots may even be able to explore inside our bodies!

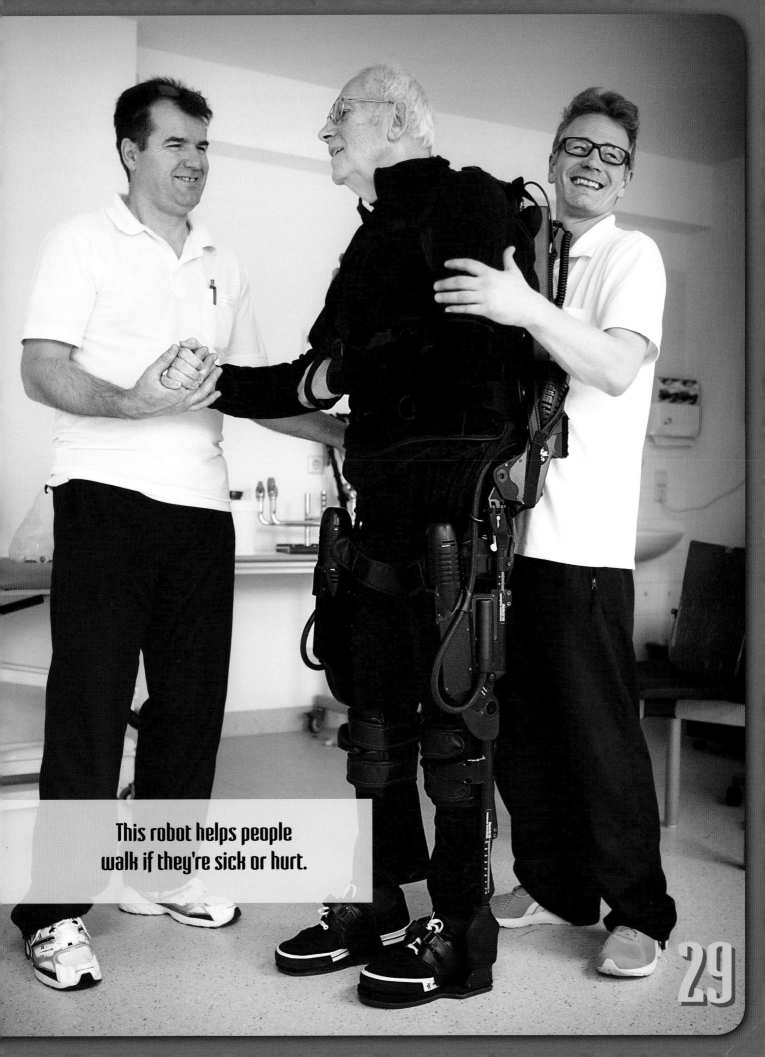

This robot helps people walk if they're sick or hurt.

29

GLOSSARY

battery: a device that turns chemical energy into electricity

competition: an event in which people try to beat others

complex: having to do with something with many parts that work together

creativity: the ability to make new things or think of new ideas

design: to create the pattern or shape of something, or the pattern created

engineering: the use of science and math to build better objects

industry: a group of businesses that provide a particular product or service

material: something used to make something

participate: to take part in something

science fiction: stories about how people and societies are affected by imaginary science discoveries and inventions

sumo: a Japanese form of wrestling that is performed by very large men

technology: the way people do something using tools and the tools that they use

FOR MORE INFORMATION

BOOKS

Baker, John R. *Astonishing Robot Competitions.* Mankato, MN: Capstone Press, 2018.

Gifford, Clive. *iRobot: Discover Extraordinary Robot Technology.* London, UK: Carlton Kids Press, 2017.

Lindeen, Mary. *Robot Competitions.* Minneapolis, MN: Lerner Publishing, 2017.

WEBSITES

NASA: Robotic Competitions
robotics.nasa.gov/events/competitions.php
Learn about more than 30 robotics competitions.

Robot Battles
robotbattles.com
Visit this website to learn about one of the oldest robot combat competitions in the world.

Robots for Kids
sciencekids.co.nz/robots.html
Watch videos, play games, and learn all about robots on this site.

INDEX